SERMON OUTLINES
on

The Grace
of God

Also by Al Bryant

Climbing the Heights
Day by Day with C. H. Spurgeon
New Every Morning
Sermon Outlines on the Attributes of God
Sermon Outlines on Christ's Death, Resurrection, and Return
Sermon Outlines on the Cross of Christ
Sermon Outlines on the Deeper Life
Sermon Outlines for Evangelistic Services
Sermon Outlines on Faith, Hope, and Love
Sermon Outlines on the Family and Home
Sermon Outlines on the Fruit of the Spirit
Sermon Outlines for Funerals and Other Special Services
Sermon Outlines on the Grace of God
Sermon Outlines on the Holy Spirit
Sermon Outlines for Lay Leaders
Sermon Outlines on the Life of Christ
Sermon Outlines on New Testament Bible Characters
Sermon Outlines on Old Testament Bible Characters
Sermon Outlines on Paul's Letter to the Romans
Sermon Outlines on Prayer and Spiritual Living, vols. 1 & 2
Sermon Outlines on Prophetic Themes
Sermon Outlines on the Psalms
Sermon Outlines on Revival Themes
Sermon Outlines for Special Occasions, vols. 1 & 2
Sermon Outlines for Worship Services

SERMON OUTLINES

on

The Grace of God

compiled by
Al Bryant

kregel
PUBLICATIONS

Grand Rapids, MI 49501

Sermon Outlines on the Grace of God by Al Bryant

Copyright © 1996 by Kregel Publications, a division of Kregel, Inc., P.O. Box 2607, Grand Rapids, MI 49501. Kregel Publications provides trusted, biblical publications for Christian growth and service. Your comments and suggestions are valued.

Library of Congress Cataloging-in-Publication Data
Bryant, Al (1926–
  Sermon outlines on the grace of God / [compiled by] Al Bryant.
    p. cm.
Includes index.
  1. Sermon outlines, syllabi, etc. I. Bryant, Al, 1926–
BV4223.S436   1996   251'.02—dc20   96-30470
                                              CIP

ISBN 0-8254-2082-2

2 3 4 5 6 / 07 06 05 04 03

Printed in the United States of America

CONTENTS

Sermon Outlines Based on New Testament Texts

PREFACE

Because the grace of God is such a broad and all-encompassing subject I have chosen to divide this collection into three more focused subject areas:

• The Grace of God
• The Goodness of God
• The Greatness of God

The poet Annie Johnson Flint said it so well:

> His love has no limit, His grace has no measure,
> His power has no boundary known unto men;
> For out of His infinite riches in Jesus
> He giveth, and giveth, and giveth again.

Fittingly, we begin with outlines drawing on Old Testament passages and progress on into the New Testament. But the theme of the grace of God permeates the Scriptures.

I hope this collection of sermon outlines will reveal and revel in the many facets of that great gem of His goodness and grace as His divine character is extolled and celebrated. I have added suitable poems* and illustrations throughout the compilation to enhance the message of these timeless outlines.

AL BRYANT

---

*The poems in this compilation are used by permission and taken from *Sourcebook of Poetry*, published in 1992 by Kregel Publications.

SCRIPTURE INDEX

"I WILL" OF GOD'S COVENANTING GRACE

The Lord covenanted with Himself that He would bless His people, and He always keeps His word. See the seven "I wills" of His pledged word in Exodus 6:6–8:

1. The **I will** of deliverance. "I will bring you out."

2. The **I will** of liberty. "I will rid you of their bondage."

3. The **I will** of power. "I will redeem you."

4. The **I will** of relationship. "I will take you to Me for a people."

5. The **I will** of friendship. "I will be to you a God."

6. The **I will** of blessing. "I will bring you into the land."

7. The **I will** of inheritance. "I will give it to you for a heritage."

F. E. Marsh

The Grace of God

When the learned and wealthy John Selden was dying he said to Archbishop Usher, "I have surveyed most of the learning that is among the sons of men, and my study is filled with books and manuscripts (he had 8000 volumes in his library) on various subjects. But at present I cannot recollect any passage out of all my books and papers whereon I can rest my soul, save this from the sacred Scriptures:

"'The grace of God that bringeth salvation hath appeared to all men, teaching us that, denying ungodliness and worldly lusts, we should live soberly, righteously, and godly, in this present world; looking for that blessed hope, and the glorious appearing of the great God and our Saviour Jesus Christ: who gave Himself for us, that He might redeem us from all iniquity, and purify unto Himself a peculiar people, zealous of good works'" (Titus 2:11–14).

A MESSAGE TO YOU

I have a message from God unto thee (Judg. 3:20).

(One makes use of the context and of an accommodated application here.)

1. **"I"**
Christ's Ministers Today Are Messengers from His People.

2. **"I have a message . . ."**
Man needs a direct message from God. "God who at sundry times and in divers manners spake in time past unto the fathers by the prophets, hath in these last days spoken unto us by his Son."

3. **"I have a message from God . . ."**
The Gospel is a message from a personal God to His children. It satisfies human longing for communion with God, appealing to our reason and sense of justice, awakening our love and giving us a worthy object for our loving. But, let us not forget that to dishonor God's message is to dishonor God himself.

4. **"I have a message from God unto thee."**
It is a *personal* message: "I have redeemed thee."
God cares for individuals. "Even the hairs of your head are all numbered." It is a suitable and satisfying message, and easily understood.
When personally appropriated, this message from God brings hope to the desponding, faith to the doubter, rest to the weary and heavy laden, comfort to the mourner, peace to the troubled, and light and life for all.

Selected

Vespers

God, who made Earth and Heaven,
    Darkness and light,
Who the day for toil hast given,
    For rest the night,
May thine angel guards defend us,
Slumber sweet thy mercy send us,
Holy dreams and hopes attend us.
    This livelong night.

—Reginald Heber

A GREAT VICTORY, BUT GOD'S

So God subdued on that day Jabin the king of Canaan before the
children of Israel (Judg. 4:23).

It was a great victory; but it was God's victory.

I. What He Did. "He subdued Jabin the king of Canaan."
    A. This is the normal result of God's activity. For God to
act is for Him to conquer. When the victory tarries it is only God
waiting.
    B. He subdued Jabin the king of Canaan. Who is able to
stand against Him? Every oppressor of God's people becomes His
foe. He who smites them virtually challenges God.

II. How He Did It. "So."
    A. By inspiring Deborah with a holy courage.
    B. By arrangement. The plan of salvation is only one grand
instance of the Divine order.

III. When He Did It. "On that day."
    God never miscalculates. The Eternal is never late.
    A. It was as soon as Israel wanted it, needed it.
    B. It was when they were most ready to receive it.

IV. Where He Did It. "Before the children of Israel."
    A. There are many things God does out of our sight.
    B. There are times and instances when He works by signs
that are visible. It was so at the Red Sea. It was so on Mount Carmel.
The victory was both decided and manifest.

Selected

The Riddle of the World

The riddle of the world is understood
Only by him who feels that God is good;
As only he can feel who makes his love
The ladder of his faith, and climbs above
On the rounds of his best instincts; draws no line
Between mere human goodness and divine.
But judging God by what in him is best,
With a child's trust leans on a Father's breast.

—John Greenleaf Whittier

GOD'S VARIED GIFTS

To every man according to his service (Num. 7:5).

The tabernacle was complete and set up. Provision was made for its safe removal from place to place as Israel journeyed. This work was assigned to the Levites. The work was graciously and wisely distributed proportionate to strength. "To every man according to his service." The Divine assignment was varied and proportionate.

Note first the fact that

1. **God Is the Source of Our Gifts and Opportunities.**
   Second, observe that

2. **God's Gifts Are Varied.**
   People differ widely in many things: physical vigor, mental capacity, education, spiritual gifts, etc. For some of these differences they are themselves largely accountable, but all discrepancies cannot be so explained. We can refer many such problems only to God's sovereign will. This truth wisely apprehended and believed would destroy a thousand seeds of discontent and envy. "Even so, Father, for so it seemed good in thy sight."

3. **God's Gifts Are Proportionate.**
   With these Levites in each case there was proportioned the means of transportation to the burden assigned. God is bountiful, but not wasteful. We possess no talents or opportunities to be counted superfluous.

4. **God Requires That We Use His Gifts and Endowments.**
   He desires the exercise of our capabilities.

5. **His Requirements Are Never Greater Than Our Endowments.**
   If we cannot give thousands we can at least devote our "two mites."

6. **But God Does Require Our Enlistment.**
   And He rewards "according to service."

Selected

GIANTS, GRAPES, AND GRASSHOPPERS

And there we saw the giants, the sons of Anak, which come of the giants: and we were in our own sight as grasshoppers, and so we were in their sight (Num. 13:33).

There is a great difference between truth and facts. This was a mean report; it was hardly a report at all; so nearly may a man come to speak the truth and yet not be truthful. The manner of their praising the land. It was with a "but." Surely it flows with milk and honey, "but." But walls; but giants; but they are strong; but we were in our own sight as grasshoppers! Giants, Grapes, Grasshoppers!

1. **God's Promises Will Always Bear Investigation.**
   He had said they should enter Canaan.

2. **There Are Anakim to Be Encountered in the Conquest of Every Promised Land.**
   "Little by little." If we decline to enter upon the conflict we shall fall short of the inheritance.

3. **The Believer Is Always Able to Conquer His Spiritual Adversaries with the Help of God.**
   It is not a question of feebleness, but of faith.

Selected

Pension For Life—And Starving

An aged Indian, half naked and famished, wandered into one of our Western settlements, begging for food to keep him from starving. While eagerly devouring the bread bestowed by the hand of charity, a bright colored ribbon, from which was suspended a small dirty pouch, was seen around his neck. On being questioned, he said it was a charm given him in his younger days: and opening it, displayed a faded, greasy paper, which he handed to the investigator for inspection. It proved to be a regular discharge from the Federal Army, entitling him to a pension for life and signed by General Washington himself.

—Selected

GOD'S PRESENCE A GUARANTEE OF A GOOD NEW YEAR

And the Lord was with him; and he prospered whithersoever he went forth (2 Kings 18:7).

In King Hezekiah we have a beautiful and powerful example of a truly prosperous man, and in him we see what are the conditions of prosperity (vv. 5–6).

I. God's Presence in the Heart Removes the Hindrances to Prosperity.
A. Sin
B. Self
C. Selfishness

II. God's Presence in the Heart Facilitates Prosperity.
It promotes
A. Spiritual growth.
B. Spiritual progress.
C. Spiritual service. Growing in grace, that growth finding expression in increased devotion and zeal and leading on to service.

III. God's Presence in the Heart Is a Guarantee of Prosperity.
A real life means real prosperity. Of this God's presence is the guarantee.

IV. God's Presence in the Heart Is the Pledge of Permanent Blessing.
If it can be said of us, "And the Lord was with him," then it will certainly be added, "and he prospered whithersoever he went forth."

Selected

LIFE'S HIDDEN MEANING
WHEN GOD IS IN CONTROL

*Days should speak, and multitude of years should teach wisdom
(Job 32:7).*

It is an optical fact that objects unequally distant cannot be seen together. So it is hard to look at the retrospective and prospective lessons of the years or to see clearly both what is temporal and near at hand and what is eternal and remote. The unspiritual man fixes his eye on the trial balance or stock exchange, but forgets the internal gallery of the immortal future. The visionary dreamer, on the other extreme, forgets the actual material world about him. The passing years call us to just and wise judgments.

1. They exalt superlative wisdom as something more than shrewdness in a narrow work.

2. They bring us to a profounder philosophy of life, showing its hidden meanings.

3. They exalt what is spiritual and eternal above the temporal and fleeting.

4. They include the tender memories and affections, but lift them into the larger vision of the soul.

5. They teach us to trust Him whose hand unrolls the future.

Selected

I Know that God Is Good

I see the wrong that round me lies,
   I feel the guilt within;
I hear, with groan and travail-cries,
   The world confess its sin.

Yet, in the maddening maze of things,
   And tossed by storm and flood,
To one fixed trust my spirit clings:
   I know that God is good!

—John Greenleaf Whittier

HOW NATURE PREACHES

The heavens declare the glory of God; and the firmament showeth his handywork (Ps. 19:1).

Nature exists not for a merely natural but for a moral end; not alone for what it is, but for what it says or declares. God looks upon nature as a basis of language. The heavenly bodies are signs. Signs are vehicles of ideas. They say something. The universe is God's telephone system, His grand signal system by which He flashes messages from the heights above to the deepest valleys below. The material system is God's great instrument of conversation. "The heavens declare the glory of God, and the firmament showeth his handywork."

1. The *fact of nature* reveals the Being of God.

2. The *vastness of nature* shows His immensity.

3. The *uniformity of nature* declares His unity.

4. The *regularity of nature* discloses His unchangeableness.

5. The *variety of nature* manifests His inexhaustibility.

6. The *adaptations of nature* unveil His wisdom.

7. The *happiness of nature* displays His goodness.

Nature tells us to think of God. God would have us contemplate nature. It is not His only revelation, but it is a very great and beautiful one. God's testimony is of both the works and the Word. Nature is a volume in which the Godhead of the Creator is plainly discoverable. Scripture is the volume in which all may read the Divine will concerning them. Study both.

Selected

TURBULENT TIMES AND GOD'S REIGN

The Lord sitteth upon the flood; yea, the Lord sitteth King forever
(Ps. 29:10).

This is a comforting text for a troubled time.

I. It Reveals to Us, First, a Turbulent Scene—a flood, which suggests:

A. Commotion. In the moral domain. Spiritually. Nationally. Internationally.

B. Innovation. Breaking down of barriers.

C. Distress. Furious and violent. The moral world is not like a river flowing on peacefully in its channel. It is "flood."

II. It Reveals, Second, a Tranquil God—"The Lord sitteth."

A. A consciousness of His right to reign. If He had any moral misgivings He would not be at ease. A usurper could not be tranquil over such a tumultuous empire.

B. A consciousness of supremacy of power to reign. No feeling of incapacity. God can control with consummate ease the whole. Rejoice.

Selected

Now I See

"Now I see!" But not the parting
  Of the melting earth and sky,
Not a vision dread and startling,
  Forcing one despairing cry.
But I see the solemn saying,
  All have sinned and all must die,
Holy precepts disobeying,
  Guilty all the world must lie.
Bending, silenced, to the dust,
Now I see that God is just.

"Now I see!" But not the glory,
  Not the face of Him I love,
Not the full and burning story
  Of the mysteries above.
But I see what God hath spoken,
  How His well-beloved Son
Kept the laws which man hath broken,
  Died for sins which man hath done;
Dying, rising, throned above!
"Now I see" that God is love.

—Frances Ridley Havergal

"GREAT THINGS"

Who hast done great things, O God (Ps. 71:19).

C. H. Spurgeon, that prince of preachers, once said: "God's mercy is so great that it forgives great sins to great sinners after great lengths of time, and then gives great favors and great privileges, and raises us up to great enjoyments in the great heaven of the great God. As John Bunyan well said, 'It must be great mercy or no mercy, for little mercy will never serve my turn.'"

Many are the great things the great God has done. The following are a few of the great things He shows us:

1. Loved with a **"Great Love"** (Eph. 2:4). His love is a fathomless ocean, a mine of wealth, a lasting spring, a glorious provision, a sun of warmth, a lifting power, and an unceasing inspiration.

2. Saved with a **"Great Salvation"** (Heb. 2:3). God is its source, man is its object, Christ is its embodiment, deliverance is its meaning, the Spirit is its power, faith is its receiver, holiness is its outcome, and glory is its consummation.

3. Thrilled with a **"Great Joy"** (Luke 2:10; Acts 8:8; 15:3). The Savior is its secret, substance, supply, and source. His joy makes our joy full and lasting.

4. Strengthened with **"Great Power"** (Acts 4:33). The Spirit's enduement is the power to keep us right, and to work in and through us with effective might.

5. Communing with **"Great Delight"** (Song of Sol. 2:3). Sitting under the shadow of His Cross, and listening to the voice of His Word, and feeding on the promises of His grace, we have "great delight" in His presence.

6. Enjoying the **"Great Peace"** of His Word (Ps. 119:165). To love God's Word is to find the joy of His grace, the tenderness of His love, the holiness of His sanctity, and the peace of His promises.

7. Expecting the **"Great Glory"** (Luke 21:27). When Christ comes to the world His saints will come with Him. He will not have the glory apart from His saints, and it would be no glory if He were not with it.

F. E. Marsh

MEDITATION ON GOD

While I was musing the fire burned (Ps. 39:3)

It is better to have too much than too little feeling in the church. We cannot love an unfeeling man. The feeling heart is the most human as well as the most humane part of humanity. But we admire it only when it leans upon a clear judgment and is thereby controlled.

There is much to be said in praise of quiet musing. We do not do much of it or see much of it in these days of rush and hurry. It has been said that meditation is a lost art. The order suggested here is musing, burning, speaking. "While I was musing the fire burned; then spake I with my tongue." Meditation is favorable to the most exalted feelings of devotion.

I. **Some proper subjects of meditation.**
  1. The character of God
  2. His providential dealings.
  3. The plan of salvation.
  4. Our relation to God.
  5. Our future.

II. **Some benefits of meditation.**
  1. The acquisition of religious power.
  2. The production of religious pleasure.
  3. The realization of religious hopes.

III. **Meditation is at its best when:**
  1. It is preparative for society and for action. We are the better fitted to go back again to our active duties and demands.
  2. We are made more kind, more gentle, more forbearing.
  3. In musing we are taught a more correct knowledge of ourselves than we should other wise possess, and may thus be fitted to have more power to correctly appraise and give aid to our neighbor.

Selected

THE SALVATION OF GOD

Restore to me the joy of your salvation and grant me a willing spirit, to sustain me (Ps. 51:12).

1. The Author of Salvation. The Lord Jesus (Heb. 5:9).

2. The Way of Salvation. Through faith (Acts 14:27).

3. The Knowledge of Salvation. By the Word (Luke 1:77).

4. The Joy of Salvation. In the believers (Ps. 51:12).

5. The Day of Salvation. Now (2 Cor. 6:2).

Salvation is of the Lord. For all who believe. The knowledge of it comes by believing the Word, and the joy of it follows.

Selected

THE CHRISTIAN'S SATISFACTION IN GOD

Thou art my portion, O Lord (Ps. 119:57).

1. God Is a Suitable Portion.

2. God Is a Satisfying Portion.

3. God Is a Universally Accessible Portion.

4. God Is an Ever-present Portion.

5. God Is an Unchanging Portion.

6. God Is an Everlasting Portion.

"Thou art my portion, O Lord." It is my supreme happiness to have it so.

Selected

CAN GOD, THE ALMIGHTY, BE LIMITED?

Again and again they turned away and tempted God to kill them, and limited the Holy One of Israel from giving them his blessings (Ps. 78:41 LB).

God's wise and benevolent purposes are often frustrated. There are many things God would do for men if permitted.

1. **Inconsistent Christian Living Handicaps God.** "Your iniquities have separated" (Isa. 59:1–2). "Your sins have withholden" (Jer. 5:25).

2. **Lack of Faith Limits God.** We limit the Holy One of Israel by distrust. Jesus at Nazareth "could there do no mighty works because of their unbelief" (Mark 6:5). Many of us lack adventurous religion. We are afraid to "launch out into the deep." When you say, "My sins are too many to be forgiven," you have limited God. You have put your sins above His grace.

3. **Shallow and Selfish Prayers Limit God.** They restrict Him. "Ye ask and receive not because ye ask amiss" (James 4:3). See the parable of the Pharisee and the publican. We often limit God by the contractedness of our prayers. Also by our lack of praying.

4. **A Stubborn Will Limits God.** "He came to his own, and his own received him not" (John 1:11). "O Jerusalem, Jerusalem, . . . how often would I have gathered thy children, but ye would not" (Matt. 23:37).

To limit God is to set bounds to His operations, to circumscribe or confine Him in His ability to effect certain purposes or works. The penitent sinner often does this when he doubts God's willingness and ability to save. The Christian in trouble often does this in confining God to a certain mode of deliverance. God extends His gifts, but we must accept them. Jesus invites us to come, but He can't compel us to come. Jesus stands at the door and knocks, but we must open the door. The key is on our side.

Selected

"OTHER REFUGE HAVE I NONE"

God is a refuge for us (Ps. 62:8).

Christians possess advantage of which unbelievers seem to be ignorant. When visited by calamity they have an unfailing Refuge in God.

1. **Our need of the Divine Refuge.** Sensible of our sin and guilt, and of our helplessness to deliver ourselves, we need and know no other refuge but God. Though the believer may know himself delivered from guilt and condemnation, he is still aware that he is not finally delivered. He dwells in a corrupt world. He still dwells in a body of sin and death. He feels deeply his need of such a refuge as God is. On account of the conflict he must wage, in his own heart and with the world, he needs a refuge.

   Not only is there sin to contend with, but no believer can be free from tribulation. "Man is born to trouble as the sparks fly upward." "Many are the afflictions of the righteous"—personal losses, poverty, family bereavements, the slander and persecutions of human tongues— all these the Christian is subject to. He needs a refuge. God is his refuge and strength. "Other refuge have I none."

2. **The nature of this refuge—the kind of refuge God is.** A refuge is a place of safe retreat. It is a place of escape from danger, where one can find protection from the pursuit of an enemy. In Old Testament times there were appointed "cities of refuge." God is such a refuge. Think of His excellency as a refuge, suitable, strong, effectual, easy of access, unfailing. When sensible of sin and guilt, in time of conflict, in tribulation, in affliction, "Other refuge have I none; hangs my helpless soul on Thee!"

3. **To enjoy this refuge we must fly to it.** We must be in it. To be only near is of no avail. When we take refuge in God He will give us grace to fight a good war, to conquer the world.

Selected

GOD HAS DONE GREAT THINGS

The Lord has done great things for us, and we are filled with joy
(Ps. 126:3 NIV).

A deep sense of our total dependence upon God as the true Source of all true enjoyment should permeate the mind of the Christian. This psalm celebrates that joy and probably commemorates the close of the Jewish Babylonian captivity.

Here, in the first place, is a

1. Very Happy Statement.

It acknowledges the Divine Hand. "The Lord hath done." God is the foundation of all good, temporal, spiritual, eternal. Whatever the streams, He is the source. "Giver of every good and perfect gift." "Great things." The Jews had long groaned under captivity. To them deliverance was a "great thing."

God has done "great things" for us, in redemption, in the bestowal of freedom—liberty to the spiritual captive, release from the guilt and power of sin. Another "great thing" received is adoption into God's family, and so made partakers of the privileges and joys of His children. Not the least of these is the enjoyment of church fellowship. Spiritual advancement, "growth in grace," is another "great thing."

It is, second,

2. A Joyful Result.

"Whereof we are glad." How glad the captive Jews when released and restored to their land and homes! The Christian can never forget past mercies, past deliverances, past benefits. The resultant joy— "whereof we are glad." "I constantly feel that you are doing great things for me. I daily and hourly enjoy them; shall I not praise you?" It is heartfelt gladness. "Bless the Lord, O my soul, and all that is within me bless his holy name!" This gladness is increased when I consider my utter unworthiness of being the recipient of such "great things."

It is also,

3. Social Gladness.

"For us." "We are glad." One design of Christian association is to remember the goodness of the Lord and to be made glad together in holy praise.

Selected

THE GOODNESS OF GOD

They will celebrate your abundant goodness . . . (Ps. 145:7 NIV).

Thanksgiving, an observatory from which to level our telescope upon the goodness of God.

I. What Is Revealed.
A. A goodness possessed.
B. A goodness shown.
C. A goodness impressive.

II. What Is Felt.
A. A "memory" of the God who is good.
B. Personal realizations.
C. A sense of gratitude—a thing so apt to fade out of mind and heart.

III. What Is Done: "Uttered."
A. Statedly.
B. Without stint.
C. In unison.
D. With reverence.
E. "Sing of." Let us today unveil a tablet to the goodness of God.

S. B. Dunn

O Little Self

O little self, within whose smallness lies
All that man was, and is, and will become,
Atom unseen that comprehends the skies
And tells the tracks by which the planets roam;
That, without moving, knows the joys of wings,
The tiger's strength, the eagle's secrecy,
And in the hovel can consort with kings,
Or clothe a God with His own mystery.
O with what darkness do we cloak Thy light,
What dusty folly gather Thee for food,
Thou who alone art knowledge and delight,
The heavenly bread, the beautiful, the good.
O living self, O God, O morning star,
Give us Thy light, forgive us what we are.

—John Masefield

GOD AND EMERGENCIES

When my soul fainted within me I remembered the Lord (Jonah 2:7).

1. A prodding shipmaster stirred up Jonah's sleeping conscience.

2. A consciousness of God dawns under various circumstances.

3. Previous experiences with God come to the rescue in a crisis.

4. Escape mechanisms to save faces are devices to escape truth and reality.

5. God is gracious and patient and guides the disgruntled prophet.

6. Spiritual retreats are vital soul needs, inspiring and urgently necessary.

7. The prophet knows God better as he reveals Him to others.

8. A prodigal prophet turns and tries God's way again.

9. God can use any and all situations for His purpose.

10. Where God and man meet, that is holy ground.

W. D. Mehrling

All I Have Is Yours

In one of Dr. J. Wilbur Chapman's meetings a man arose to give the following remarkable testimony: "I got off at the Pennsylvania depot as a tramp, and for a year I begged on the streets for a living. One day I touched a man on the shoulder and said, 'Mister, please give me a dime.'

"As soon as I saw his face, I recognized my father. 'Father, don't you know me?' I asked. Throwing his arms around me, he cried, 'I have found you; all I have is yours.' Men, think of it, that I, a tramp, stood begging my father for ten cents, when for eighteen years he had been looking for me to give me all he was worth!"

So the heavenly Father is waiting for you. Why not receive the unsearchable riches in Christ now?

—Moody Magazine

"I WILL'S" IN ISAIAH 65

God's promises and judgments are always emphatic.

1. **"I will"** of action. "I will not keep silence, but will recompense" (v. 6).

2. **"I will"** of retribution. "I will measure their former work into their bosom" (v. 7).

3. **"I will"** of compensation. "I will bring forth a seed out of Jacob, and out of Judah an inheritor of My mountains, and Mine elect shall inherit it, and My servants shall dwell there" (v. 9).

4. **"I will"** of judgment. "I will number to the sword" (v. 12).

5. **"I will"** of joy. "I will rejoice in Jerusalem, and joy in My people" (v. 19).

6. **"I will"** of answer. "I will answer" (v. 24).

7. **"I will"** of promptness. "While they are yet speaking I will hear" (v. 24).

Selected

Wealth Unclaimed

The magnificent 19th-century ten-story bank building, known as the "Society of Savings," located in Cleveland, Ohio, was built from unclaimed funds of people.

Much of this money was deposited by poor people who died. The directors of the bank, after waiting for years for these depositors to claim that which was theirs, turned the money over to the building of this beautiful bank building.

The unclaimed promises in God's Word are sufficient, and over to build spiritual edifices in life.

—Selected

Lifetime Rail Pass Goes Unused

We learned that when Crowfoot, the great chief of the Blackfoot confederacy in southern Alberta, gave the Canadian Pacific Railway permission to cross the Blackfoot land from Medicine Hat to Calgary, he was given in return a lifetime pass. Crowfoot put it in a leather case and carried it around his neck for the rest of his life. There is no record, however, that he availed himself of the right to travel anywhere on the CPR trains.

God's promises are not for decoration.

—Prairie Overcomer

OVERCOMING DISCOURAGEMENT

Comfort ye, comfort ye my people, saith your God (Isa. 40:1).

God is our help in trouble. "My" people. "Your" God. These pronouns are the key words to the whole book. When the soul is in exile or bitter pain look out for comfort.

1. It Will Come Certainly.

2. It Will Come Proportionately.
   As your needs, so your comfort.

3. It Will Come Divinely.
   God reserves to Himself the prerogative of comfort.

4. It Will Come Mediately.
   Some method or messenger of God will deliver it.

5. It Will Come Variously.
   Sometimes by a letter, a message, a visit of a friend.

6. Store Up Comfort.

This is the prophet's mission. It is ours. A noted preacher is quoted as saying near the close of his ministry that if he had his life to live over again he would preach more comforting sermons. And the only true source of comfort is God Himself.

Selected

He Holds My Hand

It isn't that I cling to Him
  Or struggle to be blest;
He simply takes my hand in His
  And there I let it rest.

So I dread not any pathway,
  Dare to sail on any sea,
Since the handclasp of Another
  Makes the journey safe for me.

—Author Unknown

THE CHIDING QUESTION

Can a maid forget her ornaments, or a bride her attire? Yet my people have forgotten me days without number (Jer. 2:32).

Consider whom Israel had forgotten. Their Father, their life, their all. God, the good, the best, one who has a supreme right to be remembered. Who were they that forgot God? Not strangers. Not heathen. But "my people." Note how sad the space of time in which they had forgotten: "days without number"—"Days and days." How long have you forgotten God, neglected Him and your duties toward Him? And how is God forgotten? Forgotten through worldliness. Forgotten through self-seeking—living unto self. Forgotten in failure to trust. In trouble, anxious, worried. Why? Because God has been forgotten in the way of His promise to help. To forget God leads to all sorts of mischief.

The chiding question is put: "Can a maid forget her ornaments, or a bride her attire?" The question is put gently, artfully yet searchingly.

We may suppose that question is asked because

1. There Are So Many Trivial Things That Occupy People's Minds.

They cannot forget them. How sad that the best things should not equally engross our thoughts!

If a bride did not remember her attire, or a maid did forget her ornaments,

2. It Would Be Very Unreasonable Behavior.

How infinitely more unreasonable it is that you or I should forget God! He is our diadem of glory. He is "the one altogether lovely." It would have been a most unreasonable thing for a bride to forget her attire at her wedding.

3. Consider the Conduct of the Maid or the Conduct of the Bride with Regard to Her Ornaments.

She labors hard to obtain her ornaments and to gain her attire. Women in the East, and their manner of gaining, placing, and retaining ornaments. They think a great deal of them. When one is lost, how diligently sought! How joyfully the Eastern woman puts on her jewels and attire!

4. Have We in Any Measure Forgotten God?

"You treat no other friend so ill." Think, if He had forgotten you.

Selected

A Quiet Mind

What room is there for troubled fear?
  I know my Lord, and He is near;
And He will light my candle, so
  That I may see the way to go.

There need be no bewilderment
  To one who goes where he is sent;
The trackless plain, by night and day
  Is set with signs lest he should stray.

My path may cross a waste of sea,
  But that need never frighten me—
Or rivers full to very brim,
  But they are open ways to Him.

My path may lead thro' wood at night,
  Where neither moon nor any light
Of guiding star or beacon shines;
  He will not let me miss my signs.

Lord, grant to me a quiet mind,
  That, trusting Thee—for Thou art kind—
I may go on without fear,
  For Thou, my Lord, art always near.

—*Amy Carmichael*

A MIGHTY FORTRESS IS OUR GOD

Get up and dress and go out and tell them whatever I tell you to say . . .
(Jer. 1:17 LB).

I. Jeremiah Commissioned as a Witness: "Speak unto them all that I command thee."

A. God's witness must be quick, ready. "Gird up thy loins." The first sign that a man is in earnest about any work is a gathering of his garments, tucking them in his belt, so as to be unhampered and free.

B. God's witness must be bold, faithful. He must speak all that he is charged with. He must speak to all whom he is charged against. Why? Because he has no reason to fear man if he be faithful.

II. Why Can He Be so Fearless?

Because a sure stronghold is God. "I have made thee this day a defensed city." Enemy attacks shall be as against an "impregnable city," as against an unshakable "iron pillar," as against a "wall of brass."

III. "They Will Fight Against Thee."

Expect opposition.

A. The vehemence of our foes.

B. The certainty of our security. The source of our confidence. God's presence. God's promise. God's power.

Selected

The Essence of Faith

Perhaps the finest of Luther's great hymns is *Ein feste Burg,* "A Mighty Fortress." Its majestic and thunderous proclamation of our faith is a singing symbol of the Reformation. Inspired by Psalm 46, Luther caught up in the hymn the very essence of faith, and the fervor and flavor of patriotism which he found in the Psalm.

Long ago in the fourteenth century, when Sergius the hermit was leading his countrymen, and Tartar hordes were overrunning his land, this Psalm was a source of strength and courage. Over and over, the godly hermit recited Psalm 46 and then led his revived men in a charge that drove the invaders back and brought ultimate victory. Throughout the ages men have been stirred by the realization that the Eternal God is available to them and that nothing, literally nothing, can overwhelm or destroy a man when he lives in this faith. *—Edward L. R. Elson*

WORSHIP ACCEPTABLE TO GOD

Your burnt offerings are not acceptable, nor your sacrifices sweet unto me (Jer. 6:20).

Then wasted worship seems possible and most unacceptable to God.

I. What was the manifest failure of these Jewish offerings?

A. By these their consecration was to be furthered; but they were foul.

B. By these their repentance was to be awakened; but they continued to sin shamefully.

C. By these their minds were to be directed to the coming Messiah; but in their attention and care for externals they lost sight of the spiritual meanings.

D. By these God was to be pleased, but the passage shows a complete miscarriage in that respect.

II. Note the indignant question and repudiation of their worship.

A. God thrusts from Himself the offensive temple offerings. He demands the heart. Nothing is sweet to God without love.

B. God stigmatizes their offerings as purposeless and waste.

C. Worship that offends God is more than waste; it is heart hardening.

D. The most important thing concerning our sacrifice of worship is its acceptableness with God.

Selected

A Heart to Praise Thee

Thou hast given so much to me,
Give one thing more—a grateful heart:
Not thankful when it pleaseth me,
As if Thy blessings had spare days,
But such a heart whose pulse may be Thy praise.

—George Herbert

GOD NIGH AT HAND

Am I a God at hand, says the Lord, and not a God afar off?
(Jer. 23:23 AMP).

There are some among us who imagine that God dwells in churches, in certain consecrated places, at certain appointed times, but who rarely think of Him as at hand. We might all wisely practice the presence of God.

I. God is nigh at hand for judgment. Our thought of judgment, therefore, need not be postponed until a remote age; every man can now bring himself within sight of the Great White Throne and can determine his destiny by his spirit and actions.

II. God is nigh at hand for protection. He is nearer to us than we can ever be to ourselves. Though the chariots of the enemy are pressing hard upon us, there is an inner circle made up of angels and ministering spirits guarding us with infinite defenses against the attacks of the foe. God does protect His people. He is near at hand for protection.

III. God is nigh at hand for inspiration. "If any man lacks wisdom, let him ask of God." What time we are in doubt or perplexity, let us whisper our need into the ear of an ever-accessible Father. He is near to prompt and inspire us, telling us by His Spirit what to do.

A. The consideration of the constant and intimate presence of God ought to encourage us in prayer, in our addresses to Him.

B. A reverential attitude should continually possess us, since God is always near with us.

C. The presence of God with us ought to deter us from all sin.

D. The presence of God with us should support us in the performance of all duty.

E. The consideration of God's nearness should comfort us in every trouble. A present Deity is a present Friend, a present Helper in every time of need.

Selected

GOD IN HUMAN ACTIVITY

And their appearance and their work was as it were a wheel in the middle of a wheel (Ezek. 1:16).

Here is a symbol of Providence. By a wheel within a wheel God governs and makes all things work together for good to those who love Him. All pleasant and all painful things. "All things." So we may put on gladness, knowing that He overrules each event of life, and while we work He works in us according to His good pleasure.

1. The Scriptures affirm this truth. They are as full of the evidences of it as the daily press is full of the records of man's workings in individual, national, and international life. Eyes see clearer washed with tears. Paul could glory in his infirmities. In all the pains and penalties, the joys and griefs, the thoughts and imaginations of life, God is busy, out of evil still bringing good.

2. History proves this. Never did men meet behind closed doors without God seeing them. Every plot and conspiracy is known to Him. There is no blind chance in the government of God or in the affairs of men. All His providences have a fixed purpose and are wisely arranged in their operation. Luther and Columbus accomplished more than they ever dreamed of because God was in their movements.

3. The laws of nature illustrate this. The thunderstorm is His scavenger, driving off the noxious vapors. The earthquake is a safety-valve by which imprisoned gases are set free.

We cannot get along without God. Nothing happens which does not help him who loves God. Losses, crosses, abuse, and injury lead to the growth of patience, watchfulness, and the silent bearing of sorrow. Burn your own smoke and go on. Trials help to build up character. Your troubles, difficulties, losses, whatever they may be and whatever may be the instruments of them, are all for God. Your times are in His hands. Your ways are ordered by Him. Your breath depends upon His will. All your sorrows and all your joys are parts of one great plan of education to make you fit to be His own forever. The government of the world is upon His shoulder and He upholds all things by the word of His power. The whole universe is ruled by God. The "whirlwind" which the prophet saw was under the throne. The wheels symbolized the government of the world in its entirety. There was an appearance "as of a wheel within a wheel," suggesting the multiform agencies and complications employed by Providence. The wheels "went straight on," thus indicating the direct course of Providence, which never halts and is never turned aside from its purposes.

Selected

God Has Time

God has time to watch the star fade
   And the sun grow dim and cold,
See the endless ages enter
   And the centuries unfold.

God has time to watch the redwood
   Grow to full maturity,
And to note the ceaseless minutes
   Nibbling at eternity.

God has time to shape the sunbeams
   And the slanting, silvery rain,
Color every flower that groweth
   And to count the amber grain.

God has time to note the falling
   Of a sparrow to the ground,
And rejoice with all His angels
   When a lost sheep has been found.

And when life's short race is finished,
   And we face the setting sun,
He'll have time to smile upon us
   And to greet us, one by one!

—Ruth M. Williams

THE PURSUING GOD

As a shepherd seeketh out his flock . . . (Ezek. 34:12).

Man is at his best when seeking God. In the kneeling attitude of man in the great quest for God we have the romance of religion. Theologically, however—

I. It Is God Seeking Man Rather Than Man Seeking God.

The history of the race is the story of God's pursuit of man. Seeking Adam and crying, "Where art thou?" Pursuing Cain (Hugo's "Conscience"). Hagar says, "Thou God seest me." Isaac is haunted by the Great Unseen. God catches the crafty Jacob and wrestles with him. Pursues Moses out into the desert. Seeks Gideon. Calls Samuel in the silent watches of the night. Goes out into the hills after David. Finds Elijah in the cave and Job on the ashheap. Pursues Saul of Tarsus. God's messengers go out into world in pursuit of souls. Paul's experiences as a pursuer (2 Cor. 11:26). Francis Thompson's "The Hound of Heaven."

II. Man Runs from God.

A. Because he is sinful. As soon as Adam sinned he began to run. The sinner hides from God.

B. Because of fear. Adam says, "I was afraid."

C. Because of foolishness. The futility of running from God (Ps. 139; Amos 9).

III. God Pursues Man.

A. Because man needs Him. God is man's greatest need.

B. Because God loves him. It is God's nature to love. So long as God loves, He will seek the sinner, and His love never fails.

C. Because He would save the sinner. God alone can satisfy, save, or restore a soul.

What a stupendous thought: Almighty God in pursuit of man!

Selected

GOD AND HIS WONDERFUL DOINGS

He is the living God, and stedfast forever, and his kingdom that which shall not be destroyed, and his dominion shall be even unto the end. He delivereth and rescueth, and he worketh signs and wonders in heaven and in earth (Dan. 6:26–27).

These are the sublime words of Darius on the preservation of Daniel in the den of the lions. Words as true as they are sublime, and words representing the most momentous principles of intelligent religion. Let us examine them, ponder them, and see what fruit they will yield, both for our mental and moral nature.

Now it is evident,

I. That Here We Have a Personal God.

He does not refer to chance or accident or mere laws. He does not refer to nature, or to natural causes and results. According to these, Daniel would have been speedily devoured by the hungry lions. But he speaks of a Divine Being—a glorious Person—One possessing wisdom, power, and dominion. In other words—a Supreme Ruler—a personal God.

But, observe, with this view of a personal deity is also given a representation,

II. Of His Certain Present Existence.

"The living God." Not a superannuated deity—not a grand effigy—not a wondrous idol or image, but a personal God, having "life." Without life there would be no available attributes of knowledge, or presence, or influence, or power. A living God is

A. *The God of nature.*

A being without conscious life could produce nothing. Not a clod of earth—not an atom of matter. But there is life in nature. Living plants—vegetable life—living animals—organic life; and to these existences of life a living God is indispensable: so also not only to give life, but to preserve and to sustain it.

B. A *living* God is *our* God.

We are endowed with the breath of lives. We have a living materialism. A mind having mental life. A soul having moral life, and these must have a living sire—a living source of being—and this is what is truly said, "In Him we live and move, and have our being."

C. A *living* God *only* can be the *object* of *worship*, *confidence*, and *hope*.

Our knowledge and faith and reverence must have respect to a living God. So praise and prayer and trust. So hope of continued life and future glory, must look up to a living God.

D. A *living* God is *essential* to the idea of *immortality*.

Only a living God can be "stedfast," or abide, as in the text. Only a living God can perpetuate His kingdom, and keep it from destruction. What could the most heroic of the ancients do, after their death? Nimrod—the mighty Nebuchadnezzar—the magnificent Solomon—the wise and illustrious! So our God is the being having in Himself unoriginated life, and who has absolute changeless being and immortality.

Then see in the text,

III. The Operations of This Living God.
Notice,

A. His *providential interpositions*.

"He delivers and rescues." Now the incident of Daniel being preserved in midst of roaring, hungry lions was a striking illustration; and here fraud and collusion were impossible: see chapters 6–8. So all history teems with instances of God's delivering and rescuing providences. As in the case of David—Jonah—the three Hebrews, etc. There is reference—

B. To the Divine *wonders* and *signs*. "Worketh signs and wonders." Now these words convey the idea of miracles and their evidences. Such as the miracle of Daniel safe in the lions' den. Now, miracle is not so much a suspension of natural law as the overruling by supernatural intervention—bringing in a direct law immediately, diverting or overruling the lower natural laws. As in the burning bush, the flame would have naturally consumed—the supernatural power preserved it though in the midst of the flame. Now, supposing material for the creation of a world had existed for unnumbered ages, and those material forces had been acting and reacting on the existing atoms—yet is it not evident that when a new state of things is to be produced, order, beauty, harmony, and life?—then the supernatural must give the mandate, and raise to higher laws than those in operation before. So creation is obviously a stupendous miracle.

All Bible revelation is built on what is implied in miracle; and the very existence of the Lord Jesus Christ, as the Son of God, rests on this basis. So says Peter in his Pentecostal sermon: "Jesus of Nazareth, a man approved of God, among you by miracles and wonders and signs, Which God did by Him in the midst of you" (Acts 2:22). Now we see the wondrous work of Christ in stilling the tempest on the Galilean lake, and the evident sign or evidence in its immediate tranquil condition. So in expelling the legion of demons, and the sign in the composure of the man's spirit as he sat at Christ's feet. In the production from a few fishes and loaves food for thousands; and in the sign given by the multitude, that they were perfectly satisfied and filled.

C. To the *moral transformation* and evidences given in the renewal of man's *nature* and *spirit*.

Observe the numberless instances around us of men and women who had been slaves of vice, bound in fetters of corruption and misery. Left to the courses of nature they would have become worse and worse. But Jesus, by His holy word and by the spirit of His grace, brought them under higher and holier influences, and now, they are new creatures, "washed, sanctified, justified," and the sign is immediately manifest in a life of purity and goodness.

Now this is the moral standing miracle of our Christianity, and is as extraordinary as any physical miracle that was ever wrought.

Learn

1. How glorious the Divine Being in whom we believe and trust. "The living God."

2. How our faith and confidence are fully justified. "He delivereth and rescueth and worketh signs."

3. How stable should be our trust, and reliant our hope, in so glorious a Being.

4. What room for all the services of worship and exercises of devotion.

Jabez Burns

GOD'S POWER

He rebukes the sea . . . (Nah. 1:3–7).

Here is a description of God's power unrivaled in sublimity. Power belongs to God. It is absolute, inexhaustible, ever and everywhere operative.

I. His Power Is Here Presented, First, as Operating in Nature.

A. It works in the air (v. 3).

B. It works in the sea. "He rebuketh the sea" (v. 4).

C. It works on the earth. "Bashan languisheth," etc. "The mountains quake," etc. (v. 4).

D. God's power is seen in all the phenomena of the material world (see Ps. 104.)

II. God's Power Is Ever Acting in the Material Universe.

It is the most philosophic explanation of all phenomena. This truth is a most hallowing aspect of the world we live in. Then walk the earth in reverence.

III. But God Is Irresistibly Against All Evil.

He is against all evildoers also. "Who can stand before his indignation?" (v. 6).

But bear in mind also:

IV. The Essential Goodness of His Character and the All-sufficiency of His Protection.

"The LORD is good, a stronghold in the day of trouble; and he knoweth them that trust in him" (v. 7).

Selected

The Big Engineer Above

Thomas Edison said: "No one can study chemistry and see the wonderful way in which certain elements combine with the nicety of the most delicate machine ever invented, and not come to the inevitable conclusion that there is a Big Engineer who is running this universe."

—Selected

THE HIDING OF GOD'S POWER

And there was the hiding place of his power (Hab. 3:4 AMP).

"It is the glory of God," says an inspired writer, "to conceal a thing." Up to a given point all is clearness. Beyond that all is mystery. This is not to promote our sense of curiosity, but is in pity for our finite powers. Concealment is a necessity. Holding back is a boon.

Habakkuk seems to have been wonderfully impressed with a sense of God's majesty and power. And well might he be. We are astonished at the exhibitions of His creative power. Even then, there is only a partial display. Omnipotence has not shown itself. More is concealed than is unfolded. We may well consider God's reserved power. "He holds back the face of his throne, and spreads a cloud about it."

I. **In the works of creation God's omnipotence is hidden.** God never makes display. In all His works we have evidence of restrained power. In nature nothing is forced to the utmost. All creation shows marks of deliberate wisdom and restrained strength. The fruits of the earth, the flowers of the garden, the season—through all nature we see "horns coming out of his hands," rays from the central sun of His omnipotence.

II. **In God's providential dealings with the race there is the hiding of His power.** All things in providence proceed according to an eternal plan. His worlds circulate. So do His providential dealings. His worlds circulate quietly and without clashing. So does His providence, gradually evolving light out of darkness, harmony out of discord, life out of death, happiness out of grief.

III. **In the revelations of spiritual truth there are hidings of God's power.** Revelation, like all other things, has been progressive. While much was given, much has been withheld for the "fulness of time." But we do not know all, though we know so much. There are fresh revelations, more knowledge to come.

IV. **In Christ's redemptive work there was the "hiding of his power."** Throughout our Savior's life there was the "hiding of his power." How remarkably free from all display was the life of Christ. His very coming to this earth was an "emptying of himself." His life was the same. His death on the cross was the same. A wonderful manifestation indeed, yet a far more wonderful concealing.

Learn

1. The hollowness of mere religious display.

2. That God has no absolute need of man's help in forwarding the interests of His kingdom.

3. Our need to get into sympathy with God.

Selected

Great God!

Great God! beneath whose piercing eye
The earth's extended kingdoms lie;
Whose favoring smile upholds them all,
Whose anger smites them, and they fall.

We bow before Thy heavenly throne;
Thy power we see, Thy greatness own;
Yet, cherished by Thy milder voice,
Our bosoms tremble and rejoice.

Thy kindness to our fathers shown
Their children's children long shall own;
To Thee, with grateful hearts, shall raise
The tribute of exulting praise.

Great God, our Guardian, Guide and Friend!
O still Thy sheltering arm extend;
Preserved by Thee for ages past,
For ages let Thy kindness last!

—William Roscoe

GOSPEL'S THREEFOLD MESSAGE

The gospel is a threefold message.

1. It is "the **gospel of the grace of God**" (Acts 20:24), proclaiming His favor to the undeserving.

2. It is the **gospel of power,** telling out the good news that God never asks us to do a thing without giving us the power to do it (Rom. 1:16).

3. It is a **gospel of glory,** declaring a better state of things in the future (2 Cor. 4:14).

Selected

Buried Thy Sins

In the deep silent depths far away from the shore,
Where they never shall rise to trouble thee more,
Where no far-reaching tide with its powerful sweep
May stir the dark waves of forgetfulness deep,
     I have buried them there—
     Where no mortal can see!
     I have cast all thy sins
     In the depths of the sea!

In the depths, in the depths, where the storm cannot come,
Where its faint echo falls like a musical drum,
Where no mortal can enter, thy faults to deride—
For above them forever flows love's mighty tide!
     In the sepulchral vaults
     Of which God holds the key!
     He has buried thy sins
     In the depths of the sea!

—Author Unknown

GOD'S GLORIOUS KINGDOM ON EARTH

Thy kingdom come. Thy will be done, as in heaven, so on earth (Matt. 6:10 ARV).

This familiar passage of Scripture (the Lord's Prayer) reminds us of how thoroughly God's heavenly kingdom permeates our daily existence as we serve Him on earth.

1. **The Kingdom of Heaven on Earth Comes First in Human Hearts as an Unforgettable Experience of God and His Love.**

   It cannot be seen unless it shines in men's faces and shows in their lives. Such persons Paul called "sons of God." They might be called "citizens of the kingdom of God."

2. **Next, the Kingdom Comes in Family Circles Where God Is an Unseen Guest.**

   The members of the circle—husband, wife, children, and treasured grandparents—live by the law of love.

3. **Then the Kingdom, Still Unseen and Working from Within Comes Like Leaven (as Christ said).**

   It is like the growth of a tree which builds from within, begins to refashion social institutions, communities, the nation, and the world, and will make them finally "the kingdom of our Lord, and of his Christ." The kingdom of God on earth will come, a civilization which centers its vast energies and its enthusiasm on human welfare.

4. **How Heartening That Long Before This Reign of God Can Be Realized in Human Society It Can Come Fully and Gloriously in Our Own Lives.**

   It comes in the little home circles about our firesides and in our churches!

Am I a citizen of the kingdom of God? Is my household ruled by love? Am I one of the builders of the Christian civilization?

Worth M. Tippy

1. **Transferred** from death to life by grace (John 5:24).

2. **Transfigured** by the Spirit by looking at Christ (2 Cor. 3:18 R.V.).

3. **Translated** by the power of God at Christ's return (Heb. 11:5).

4. **Transformed** by the Savior, and made like to Him (Phil. 3:20–21).

F. E. Marsh

Spurgeon's Worst Sermon

Mr. Spurgeon once preached what in his judgment was one of his poorest sermons. He stammered and floundered, and when he got through he felt that it had been a complete failure. He was greatly humiliated, and when he got home he fell on his knees and said, "Lord, God, You can do something with nothing. Bless that poor sermon."

And all through the week he uttered that prayer. He woke up in the night and prayed about it. He determined that the next Sunday he would redeem himself by preaching a great sermon. Sure enough, the next Sunday, the sermon went off beautifully. At the close the people crowded about him and covered him with praise. Spurgeon went home pleased with himself, and that night he slept like a baby. But he said to himself, "I'll watch the results of those two sermons." What were they?

From the one that has seemed a failure he was able to trace forty-one conversions. And from that magnificent sermon he was unable to discover that a single soul was saved. The Spirit of God used the one and did not use the other. We can do nothing without the Spirit who helps our infirmities.

—Christian Digest

CONCERNING THE FORBEARANCE OF GOD

Or despisest thou the riches of His goodness and forbearance and longsuffering; not knowing that the goodness of God leadeth thee to repentance? (Rom. 2:4).

It is an instance of divine condescension that the Lord reasons with men and asks this question and others like it (Isa. 1:5; 55:2; Jer. 8:4; Ezek. 33:11).

It is a sad thing that any who have seen God's judgments on others and have escaped themselves should draw from this special mercy a reason for adding sin to sin (Jer. 3:8).

I. Let Us Honor the Lord's Goodness and Forbearance.

A. It is manifested to us in a threefold form—
Goodness which has borne with past sin (Ps. 78:38).
Forbearance which bears with us in the present (Ps. 103:10).
Longsuffering which, in the future as in the past and the present, is prepared to bear with the guilty (Luke 13:7–9).

B. It is manifested in its excellence by three considerations—
The person who shows it. It is "the goodness *of God*" who is omniscient to see sin, just to hate it, powerful to punish it, yet patient toward the sinner (Ps. 145:8).
The being who receives it. It is dealt out to man—a guilty, insignificant, base, provoking, ungrateful being (Gen. 6:6).
The conduct to which it is a reply. It is love's response to sin. Often God forbears, though sins are many, wanton, aggravated, daring, repeated, etc. (Mal. 3:6).

II. Let Us Consider How It May Be Despised.

A. By claiming it as our due and talking as if God were bound to bear with us.

B. By perverting it into a reason for hardness of heart, presumption, infidelity, and further sin (Zeph. 1:12; Eccl. 8:11).

C. By urging it as an apology for procrastination (2 Peter 3:3–4).

III. Let Us Feel the Force of Its Leading.

A. He is not hard and unloving or He would not have spared us.

B. To go on to offend would be cruel to Him and disgraceful to ourselves. Nothing can be baser than to make forbearance a reason for provocation.

C. It is evident from His forbearance that He will rejoice to accept us if we turn to Him. He spares that He may save.

The forbearance and longsuffering of God toward sinners is truly astonishing. He was longer in destroying Jericho than in creating the world. —BENJAMIN BEDDOME

According to the proverb of the Jews, "Michael flies but with one wing, and Gabriel with two"; God is quick in sending angels of peace, and they fly apace; but the messengers of wrath come slowly. God is more hasty to glorify His servants than to condemn the wicked. —JEREMY TAYLOR

C. H. Spurgeon

Discovery

Scientific proof of how I know
That God concerns Himself with me?
Can finite eye glimpse heaven's glow?
Is there a light for man to see?
Can I be certain of the way?
May I know truth in essence pure?
Does God reveal Himself today?
Do love, and truth, and man endure?
By tube or scale, I cannot place
My faith in laboratory test
To prove God's loving, proffered care,
But in His word, I see His face
And hear His voice; and what is best,
My soul responds to find Him there.

—Carlton Buck

THE CERTAINTY OF GOD

If God be for us, who can be against us? (Rom. 8:31).

Paul staked everything on his faith expressed in this rhetorical question. It was not a gamble to him—it was an unblemished certainty! "The apostle would not argue about the nature of this God. This was the God and Father of our Lord Jesus Christ; not an impersonal factor in the cosmic process, but living, loving, just, and wise, all glorious forever.

I. The Words Suggest a Conflict.

Paul had a profound belief in the existence of evil spirits and in their power to destroy (Eph. 2:2; also 6:12). Today, for a great many, the same truth is conveyed in other ways. For example, there are certain aspects of our nature, destructive and deceptive, which demand control and even combat.

There are attitudes of the mind that ruin one's hopes of the higher life. Explain them as you may, there are forces in life that lie in wait to destroy.

Over against that put all that we know of nature's benevolence in creative activity, the love, beauty, and justice that shine from the sky, and you have evidence of that other aspect of life that prophesies the good. None of us can avoid that struggle.

II. There Is a Challenge in Paul's Words.

Earlier religions had erred in one of two directions: first, some had worshiped these destructive forces. Such religions were a "sublimated biology"; and second, some had recourse to asceticism with utter annihilation of all such life forces.

Paul's argument is that neither of these is necessary or even feasible. If God be for us, then there are no more enemies to be feared. The very forces that terrified will be made to serve Him; they will be caught up into His purpose and will be given a place in the organic process of His kingdom.

This is a challenge to unbelief, despair, and carelessness, but it must be your challenge.

III. But Take Note of the Condition So Clearly Expressed.

"If God be for us." God's conditions are not hard, for it is He, and not we, who makes them. The believing mind, the surrendered will, and the consecrated spirit—these are essential to God's presence and help. Christ shows us how to be sure. There was no "if" in his fellowship with God. Take God at His word, then, with all your heart and prove how great a Conqueror He is!

Selected

God's Presence

But God is never so far off
    As even to be near
He is within; our spirit is
    The home He holds most dear.

To think of Him as by our side
    Is almost as untrue
As to remove His throne beyond
    Those skies of starry blue.

So all the while I thought myself
    Homeless, forlorn, and weary.
Missing my joy, I walked the earth,
    Myself God's sanctuary.

I come to Thee once more, my God!
    No longer will I roam;
For I have sought the wide world thro'
    And never found a home.

Though bright and many are the spots
    Where I have built a nest—
Yet in the brightest still I pined
    For more abiding rest.

For Thou hast made this wondrous soul
    All for Thyself alone;
Ah! send Thy sweet transforming grace
    To make it more Thine own.

—Frederick William Faber

GOD'S PROMISES

For all the promises of God in Him are yea, and in Him amen, unto the glory of God by us (2 Cor. 1:20).

I. The Dignity of the Promises. They are "the promises of God."

A. They were each one made by Him according to the purpose of His own will.

B. They are links between His decrees and His acts; being the voice of the decree, and the herald of the act.

C. They display the qualities of Him who uttered them. They are true, immutable, powerful, eternal, etc.

D. They remain in union with God. After the lapse of ages, they are still His promises as much as when He first uttered them.

II. The Range of the Promises. "*All* the promises."

A. They are found both in the Old and New Testaments; from Genesis to Revelation, running through centuries of time.

B. They are of both sorts—conditional and unconditional: promises to certain works and promises of an absolute order.

C. They are of all kinds of things—bodily and spiritual, personal and general, eternal and temporal.

D. They contain blessings to varied characters, such as—
> The *Penitent*: Lev. 26:40–42; Isa. 55:7, 57:15; Jer. 3:12–13.
> The *Believing*: John 3:16, 18; 6:47; Acts 16:31; 1 Peter 2:6.
> The *Serving*: Ps. 37:3; Prov. 3:9–10; Acts 10:35.
> The *Praying*: Isa. 45:11; Lam. 3:25; Matt 6:6; Ps. 145:18.
> The *Obeying*: Ex. 19:5; Ps. 119:1–3; Isa. 1:19.
> The *Suffering*: Matt. 5:10–12; Rom. 8:17; 1 Peter 4:12–14.

III. The Stability of the Promises. "All the promises *in Him are yea, and in Him amen.*"

A Greek word "yea," and a Hebrew word "amen," are used to mark certainty, both to Gentile and Jew.

A. Their stability is in Christ Jesus beyond all hazard: for He is—

The *witness* of the promise of God,

The *surety* of the covenant,

The *sum* and *substance* of all the promises,

The *fulfillment* of the promises, by His actual incarnation,

His atoning death, His living plea, His ascension power, etc.

IV. The Result of the Promises. "The glory of God by us."

A. We glorify His condescending love in making the promise.

B. We glorify His power as we see Him keeping the promise.

C. We glorify Him by our faith, which honors His veracity, by expecting the blessings which He has promised.

D. We glorify Him in our experience which proves the promise true.

A speaker at the Fulton Street prayer meeting said, "I count all checks as cash when I am making up my money and striking a balance"; and so, when we feel that we have not much of this world's goods, we can at least take hold of God's promises, for they are just so many drafts at sight upon divine mercy, and we may count them among our possessions. Then we shall feel rich, and the soul is rich who trusts God's Word and takes His promises as something for present use.

Promises are like the clothes we wear; if there is life in the body they warm us, but not otherwise. When there is living faith the promise will afford warm comfort, but on a dead, unbelieving heart it lies cold and ineffectual. It has no more effect than pouring a cordial down the throat of a corpse. —WILLIAM GURNELL

It is when these promises are reduced to experience—when they are seen cleansing us from all filthiness of flesh and spirit, making us partakers of the divine nature, leading us to walk worthy of the vocation wherewith we are called, filling us with kindness and benevolence, supporting us cheerfully under all our trials—it is then they glorify God "by us." —WILLIAM JAY

C. H. Spurgeon

FUNDAMENTALS OF OUR FAITH

God was in Christ, reconciling the world unto himself (2 Cor. 5:19).

There is an irreducible minimum for life in every realm. Our faith demands the following things:

I. The Sovereignty of God.

Three old words may serve us well today—omniscience, omnipresence, and omnipotence. The world needs not demigods but God—merciful, almighty, and eternal.

II. The Supremacy of Jesus.

He is the final revelation of God, the anointed Savior of the world, and the Lord of a kingdom of love and righteousness as wide as the universe.

III. The Certainty of Christian Experience.

Salvation is His gift received by faith, and the church is the fellowship of the redeemed. The identity of this experience is established in the Word of God and has been confirmed by the Holy Spirit in unbroken succession through the ages. The sovereign God still saves men and women through His Son Jesus Christ.

Selected

Lord, Give Me Faith

Lord, give me faith!—to live from day to day,
With tranquil heart to do my simple part,
And, with my hand in Thine, just go Thy way.

Lord, give me faith—to trust, if not to know;
With quiet mind in all things Thee to find,
And child-like, go where Thou wouldst have me go.

Lord, give me faith!—to leave it all to Thee,
The future is Thy gift, I would not lift
The veil Thy love has hung 'twixt it and me.

—Author Unknown

THE RICHNESS OF GOD'S GRACE

But God, who is rich in mercy, for his great love wherewith he loved us, even when we were dead in sins, hath quickened us together with Christ, (by grace ye are saved;) and hath raised us up together, and made us sit together in heavenly places in Jesus Christ: that in the ages to come he might shew the exceeding riches of his grace in his kindness toward us through Christ Jesus (Eph. 2:4–7).

What a constellation of sublime ideas is here presented! We scarcely know which to admire more, the grace of the Benefactor or the richness of His gifts. Consider the richness of Divine grace.

I. In Its Formation: Richness.

God is "rich in mercy and of great love." Exhaustless springs of mercy and love in the heart of God. They have flowed down to the most unworthy of the human race. They will flow undiminished. "God is love." Source of all the grace displayed toward man.

II. In Its Streams: Richness.

The grace of God has been displayed toward us in ten thousand ways.

A. God "has quickened us even when we were dead in sins." He quickened us by that same Spirit whereby He raised Christ from the dead. What an astonishing instance of Divine grace was this!

B. He has also "raised us up and enthroned us together with Christ in heaven." The apostle had before spoken of what the Father had wrought for Christ. He now draws a parallel between believers and Christ. What was done for Christ our head was done for all the members of His body. In this view Christians may be considered risen with Christ, and already seated on His throne.

III. In Its Issue: Richness.

All ages to the end of time must admire the grace of God toward both the Jewish and the Gentile world. Everyone who partakes of that grace must of necessity admire it. "The exceeding riches of it" are unsearchable. God's kindness enhanced by flowing "through Jesus Christ." The price paid by Christ will to all eternity endear to us the purchased blessing.

Selected

MEASURING THE IMMEASURABLE

Eph. 3:16–19

He would have us measure the immeasurable, but He would first have us made fit to do so. We shall make our chief point the fourfold measurement, but we shall note that which comes before, and that which follows after.

I. The Previous Training Required for This Measurement.

A. He would have their spiritual faculties vigorous.

"Your inner man": understanding, faith, hope, love, all need power from a divine source.

"By His Spirit." The power required is spiritual, holy, heavenly, divine, actually imparted by the Holy Spirit.

B. He would have the subject always before them.

"That Christ may dwell in your heart by faith."

"In your heart." Love must learn to measure Christ's love.

It is revealed to the heart rather than to the head.

"By faith." A carnal man measures by sight, a saint by faith.

C. He would have them exercised in the art of measurement.

"That ye, being rooted and grounded in love," etc.

We must love Him ourselves, if we would measure Christ's love.

II. The Measurement Itself.

A. *The breadth.* Immense.

Comprehending all nations. "Preach the gospel to every creature."

Covering hosts of iniquities. "All manner of sin."

Compassing all needs, cares, etc.

Conferring boundless blessings for this life and worlds to come.

B. *The length.* Eternal.

Eternal love in the fountain. Election and the covenant.

Ceaseless love in the flow. Redemption, calling, perseverance.

Endless love in endurance. Longsuffering, forgiveness, faithfulness, patience, immutability.

Boundless love, in length exceeding our length of sin, suffering, backsliding, age, or temptation.

C. *The depth*. Incomprehensible.

Stoop of divine love, condescending to consider us, to commune with us, to receive us in love, to bear with our faults, and to take us up from our low estate.

Stoop of love personified in Christ.

He stoops, and becomes incarnate; endures our sorrows; bears our sins; and suffers our shame and death.

Where is the measure for all this?

Our weakness, meanness, sinfulness, despair, make one factor of the measurement.

His glory, holiness, greatness, deity, make up the other.

D. *The height*. Infinite.

As developed in present privilege, as one with Jesus.

As to be revealed in future glory.

As never to be fully comprehended throughout the ages.

III. The Practical Result of This Measurement. "That you might be filled with all the fullness of God."

Here are words full of mystery, worthy to be pondered.

Be *filled*. What great things man can hold!

Filled *with* God. What exaltation!

Filled with the *fullness* of God. What must this be?

Filled with *all* the fullness of God. What more can be imagined?

In the gospel history we find that Christ had a fourfold entertainment among the sons of men; some received Him into house, not into heart, as Simon the Pharisee who gave Him no kiss, nor water to wash His feet; some received Him into heart, but not into house, as Nicodemus, and others; some neither into heart nor house, as the graceless, swinish Gergesenes; some both into house and heart, as Lazarus, Mary, Martha.

And thus let all good Christians do; endeavor that God in Christ may dwell in their hearts by faith, that their bodies may be fit temples of His Holy Spirit, that now in this life, while Christ stands at the door of their hearts, knocking for admission, they will lift up the latch of their souls, and let Him in; for if ever they expect to enter into the gates of the city of God hereafter, they must open their hearts, the gates of their own city, to Him here in this world.

—JOHN SPENCER

"The wider the diameter of light, the greater is the circumference of darkness." The more a man knows, he comes at more points into contact with the unknown.

C. H. Spurgeon

Out in the Fields with God

The little cares that fretted me,
  I lost them yesterday,
Among the fields above the sea,
  Among the winds at play,
Among the lowing of the herds,
  The rustling of the trees,
Among the singing of the birds,
  The humming of the bees.

The foolish fears of what might happen,
  I cast them all away
Among the clover-scented grass,
  Among the new-mown hay,
Among the husking of the corn,
  Where drowsy poppies nod,
Where ill thoughts die and good are born—
  Out in the fields with God.

—Elizabeth Barrett Browning

OUR NEED AND THE DIVINE SUPPLY

*My God will supply all your need, according to his riches in glory by
Christ Jesus (Phil. 4:19).*

1. The Need of Christians.

"All your need." Your need as a sinner. As a traveler—
"pilgrim"—across the desert of the world. As a voyager across the
rough and boisterous sea of life. As a racer—stimulus and strength.
As a soldier—foes are legion. Will he be triumphant then? Yes, for:

II. God Will Supply All Your Need. Source of supply: "out of his riches in glory."

"Riches in glory"—inexhaustible treasures, abundant stores
of grace.

"Riches of glory" is a glorious phrase. It means "the fullness of God." Treasures of the Bank of Heaven.

III. The Medium of Supply—"by Christ Jesus."

All the riches of God's grace and the splendors of an eternal
heaven are to be given through Christ.

Selected

What We Have in Christ

A love that can never be fathomed;
A life that can never die;
A righteousness that can never be removed;
A peace that can never be understood;
A rest that can never be disturbed;
A joy that can never be diminished;
A hope that can never be disappointed;
A glory that can never be clouded;
A light that can never be darkened;
A happiness that can never be interrupted;
A strength that can never be enfeebled;
A purity that can never be defiled;
A beauty that can never be marred;
A wisdom that can never be baffled;
Resources that can never be exhausted.

—Selected

FILLED TO THE FULL

That ye might be filled with all the fullness of God (Eph. 3:19).

I. In What Respects May We Be Filled with All the Fullness of God?

A. In filling the heart God empties it of its former occupants.

B. In filling the heart God takes possession of it personally.

C. In filling the heart God replenishes it with all the graces and dispositions of the Christian character.

D. In filling the heart God replenishes it with every grace completely or perfectly.

II. By What Means May We Be Filled with All the Fullness of God?

A. By being sensible of our emptiness.

B. By abounding in prayer.

C. By cherishing love to Christ.

D. By following hard after God.

Selected

The Stammering Tongue

One day during his great mission in London, Mr. Moody was holding a meeting in a theater packed with a most select audience. Noblemen and noblewomen were there in large numbers, and a prominent member of the royal family was in the royal box

Mr. Moody arose to read the Scripture lesson. He attempted to read Luke 4:27: "And many lepers were in Israel in the time of Eliseus the prophet." When he came to the name of Eliseus he stammered and stuttered over it. He went back to the beginning of the verse and began to read again, but when he reached the word "Eliseus" he could not get over it. He went back the third time, but again the word was too much for him. He closed the Bible with deep emotion and looked up and said, "Oh, God, use this stammering tongue to preach Christ crucified to these people."

The power of God came upon him, and one who heard him then and had heard him often at other times said to me that he had never heard Mr. Moody pour out his soul in such a torrent of eloquence as he did then, and the whole audience was melted by the power of God.

—*Sunday School Times*

GRACE

The grace of God (Titus 2:11).

Pascal sings of grace. "To make a man a saint, grace is absolutely necessary, and whoever doubts it does not know what a saint is or what a man is."

The following blessings, mentioned in Ephesians, which grace bestows will speak for themselves.

1. We are **accepted** in the Beloved to the "praise of the glory of His grace" (1:6).

2. We are **forgiven** "according to the riches of His grace" (1:7).

3. We are "**saved** by grace," that is, through His loving act, irrespective of what we are (2:5, 8).

4. We are **made trophies** of His love through "the exceeding riches of His grace" (2:7).

5. We are privileged to be **witnesses** of the Lord through the "grace given" (3:7–8).

6. We are **exhorted** to be channels of blessings to others by a consistent life, that we may "minister grace" to them (4:29).

7. The benediction of love is, "**Grace** be with all who love our Lord Jesus Christ" (6:24).

F. E. Marsh

Newton's Prayer Prelude

Two or three years before the death of John Newton, when his sight was so dim that he was no longer able to read, a friend and brother in the ministry called to have breakfast with him. Their custom was to read the Word of God following mealtime, after which Newton would make a few short remarks on the biblical passage, and then appropriate prayer would be offered. That day, however, there was silence after the words of Scripture, "by the grace of God I am what I am," were read.

Finally, after several minutes, Newton spoke, "I am not what I ought to be! How imperfect and deficient I am! I am not what I wish to be, although I abhor that which is evil and would cleave to what is good! I am not what I hope to be, but soon I shall be out of mortality, and with it all sin and imperfection. Though I am not what I ought to be, nor what I wish to be, nor yet what I hope to be, I can truly say I am not what I once was: a slave to sin and Satan. I can heartily join with the apostle and acknowledge that by the grace of God I am what I am!" Then, after a pause, he said, "Now let us pray!"

—Our Daily Bread

GOD'S KNOWLEDGE OF HIS OWN

The Lord knows them that are his (2 Tim. 2:19).

The word "know" implies a great deal more than mere knowledge of their existence. It is an intimate matter.

1. He Knows Who They Are.

He knows them in business, in play, in devotional exercises. He knows them awake and asleep. He knows all about them—names, circumstances, weaknesses, strength.

2. He Loves Them.

He has made them what they are, renewed them in His own image. He pronounces the second, as the first creation, good. He delights in them.

3. He Guides Them.

He knows the way they take. He leads them into the paths of duty, usefulness, peace.

4. He Guards Them.

He defends and protects them, takes care of them. He is their "sun and shield." He is their "ever present help in time of trouble." They are secure.

5. He Will Hereafter Acknowledge Them.

He will vindicate their character. He will own them as His. He will receive them to Himself forever.

Our correlative obligations—to act ever as in His presence—to love and trust and praise Him at all times—to feel safe and happy— to live in the glad hope of glory.

Selected

God's Guidance

When the missionary Barnabas Shaw was forbidden to preach in Cape Town he decided not to leave Africa, but to push into the interior. He bought a yoke of oxen, put his wife and his goods into a wagon and started out, resolved to settle wherever he would be allowed to preach.

So they journeyed for three hundred miles. Then while camping one night they discovered that a band of Hottentots were also camping nearby. In conversation with the leader, Shaw learned that the heathen were on their way to Cape Town to find a missionary. The similar meeting of Philip and the eunuch (Acts 8:26–40) flashed through his mind when he realized that God had been leading him where He wanted him to go. —*Gospel Herald*

MORE AND MORE

But he gives more grace (James 4:6).

Practical as is the Epistle of James, the apostle does not neglect to extol the grace of God, as do some preachers in these times.

We err if we commend the fruits regardless of the root from which they spring. Every virtue should be traced to grace.

I. Observe the Text in Its Connection.

A. It presents a contrast. "But he gives more grace."

Two potent motives are confronted. "The spirit that dwelleth in us lusteth to envy"; on God's part this is met by, "but He giveth more grace."

B. It suggests a note of admiration.

When we discover more of our weakness, God gives more grace.

C. We learn where to obtain the weapons of our warfare: we must look to Him who gives grace.

D. It encourages us to continue the conflict.

As long as there is one passion in the believing soul that dares to rise, God will give grace to struggle with it.

E. It plainly indicates a victory.

"He gives more grace" is a plain promise that—

God will not give us up; but that He will more and more augment the force of grace, so that sin must and shall ultimately yield to its sanctifying dominion.

II. Observe the General Truth of the Text.

God is ever on the giving hand. The text speaks of it as the Lord's way and habit: "He gives more grace."

This should be—

A. A truth of daily use for ourselves.

B. A promise daily pleaded for others.

C. An assurance in prospect of the severe tests of sickness and death.

III. Bring It Home by Special Appropriation.

A. My spiritual poverty, then, is my own fault, for the Lord gives more grace to all who believe for it.

B. My spiritual growth will be to His glory, for I can only grow because He gives more grace. Oh, to grow constantly!

When Matthew Henry was a child he received much impression from a sermon on the parable of the "mustard seed." On returning home, he said to his younger sister, "I think I have received a grain of grace." It was the seed of the Commentary "cast upon the waters."

—CHARLES STANFORD

I have grace every day! every hour! When the rebel is brought, nine times a day, twenty times a day, for the space of forty years, by his prince's grace, from under the ax, how fair and sweet are the multiplied pardons and reprievals of grace to Him! In my case here are multitudes of multiplied redemptions! Here is plenteous redemption! I defile every hour, Christ washes; I fall, grace raises me; I come this day, this morning, under the rebuke of justice, but grace pardons me; and so it is all along, till grace puts me into heaven.

—SAMUEL RUTHERFORD

A little grace will bring us to heaven *hereafter*, but great grace will bring heaven to *now*.

—ARNOLD DIVINE

C. H. Spurgeon

O God, I Need Thee!

O God, I need Thee!
When morning crowds the night away
And the tasks of waking seize my mind,
I need Thy Poise,

O God, I need Thee!
When clashes come with those
Who walk the way with me,
I need Thy Smile.

O God, I need Thee!
When the path to take before me lies,
I see it—courage flees—
I need Thy Faith.

O God, I need Thee!
When the day's work is done,
Tired, discouraged, wasted;
I need Thy Rest.

—Author Unknown

GOD'S GRACE PROCLAIMED IN
JUDE'S DOXOLOGY

Now unto Him that is able to keep you from falling and to present you faultless before the presence of His glory with exceeding joy, to the only wise God our Savior, be glory and majesty, dominion and power, both now and ever. Amen" (Jude 24–25).

I. Let Us Adore Him Who Can Keep Us from Falling.

A. We need keeping from falling, in the sense of preservation from—

Error of doctrine; which is rife enough in this age.

Error of spirit: such as want of love, or want of discernment, or unbelief, or credulity, or fanaticism, or conceit.

Outward sin. Alas, how low may the best fall!

B. None but the Lord can keep us from falling.

We cannot keep ourselves without Him.

No place guarantees security: the church, the closet, the communion table—all are invaded by temptation.

No rules and regulations will secure us from stumbling. Stereotyped habits may only conceal deadly sins.

C. The Lord can do it. He is "able to keep," and He is "the only wise God, our Savior." His wisdom is part of His ability.

By warning us: this may be done by our noting the falls of others, or by inward monitions, or by the Word.

By providence, affliction, etc., which remove occasions of sinning.

By a bitter sense of sin, which makes us dread it as a burnt child dreads the fire.

By His Holy Spirit, renewing in us desires after holiness.

II. Let Us Adore Him Who Will Present Us in His Courts Faultless.

A. None can stand in those courts who are covered with fault.

B. None can deliver us from former guilt, or keep us from daily faultiness in the future, but the Savior Himself.

C. He will do it. We should not be exhorted to praise Him for an ability which He would not use.

D. He will do it "with exceeding joy," both to Himself and to us.

III. Let Us Adore Him with Highest Ascriptions of Praise.

A. Wishing Him glory, majesty, dominion, and power.

B. Ascribing these to Him as to the past, for He is "before all time" (RV).

C. Ascribing them to Him "now."

D. Ascribing them to Him "forever."

We cannot stand a moment longer than God upholds us; we are as a staff in the hand of a man; take away the hand, the staff falls to the ground: or rather, as a little infant in the nurse's hand (Hos. 11:3); if we are left to our own feet, we shall soon fall. Created grace will never hold out against so many difficulties.

Philip Dickerson, an aged Baptist minister, who died October 22, 1882, just before his death, said, "Seventy years ago the Lord took me into His service without a character. He gave me a good character, and by His grace I have kept it."

C. H. Spurgeon